Contents

KT-455-968

The ancient Romans

All human beings need food and shelter to survive. They also need a system of beliefs which gives shape and meaning to their lives. Throughout history, people have developed different ways of meeting these basic needs. By studying the people of the **Roman Empire**, we can learn how they used the resources around them to create a sophisticated way of life, many traces of which survive to this day.

IN THIS BOOK, we look at the **civilization** of the ancient Romans, a people of Italian origin. Two thousand years ago they conquered most of Europe, North Africa and the Middle East, creating one of the biggest empires in the world.

△ *Underwater archaeologists have explored many Roman shipwrecks in the Mediterranean Sea. By examining the cargo, they can tell what people ate, drank and traded.*

WE KNOW ABOUT THE ROMANS thanks to the many books and letters which have survived from their time. The remains of Roman cities, villas, forts and shipwrecks also help **archaeologists** to build up a picture of daily life in the Roman Empire.

THE EARLIEST ROMAN HISTORY is not known, so the Romans made up stories to fill in the gaps. They used the ancient legend of Romulus and Remus to explain how their city was founded. Legend has it that they were the twin sons of Mars, the god of war. They were abandoned at birth and rescued by a she-wolf. Romulus later became the first king of Rome and the city was named after him.

ROME was founded in 753 BC as a tiny farming settlement on the banks of the River Tiber. At the time, Italy was a land of many different peoples, speaking different languages. There were the **Etruscans** and Umbrians north of Rome, and Greek settlers in the south. The very first Romans belonged to the **Latin**-speaking peoples of central Italy.

▽ *Today, statues of Romulus and Remus and the she-wolf can be seen all over Rome and other Italian cities.*

MAKE it WORK!

THE ROMAN EMPIRE

Author: Peter Chrisp

Consultant: Simon James BSc, PhD
The British Museum, London

Series creator: Andrew Haslam

In association with
FRANKLIN WATTS

Created by:
Two-Can Publishing Ltd
346 Old Street
London
EC1V 9NQ

Editor: Jacqueline McCann
Art direction and design: Helen McDonagh
Managing Editor: Christine Morley
Commissioned photography: Jon Barnes
Additional photography: John Englefield and Ray Moller
Picture Research: Lyndsey Price
Production: Joya Bart-Plange
Model-maker: Melanie Williams
Additional model-makers: Peter Griffiths, Corina Holzherr, Paul Holzherr

Copyright © Two-Can Publishing Ltd, 1996
Series concept and original design © Andrew Haslam

All rights reserved. No part of this publication may be reproduced, stored
in a retrieval system or transmitted in any form or by any means electronic,
mechanical, photocopying, recording or otherwise, without prior written
permission of the copyright owner.

This edition published 1996 in association with:
Franklin Watts
96 Leonard Street
London
EC2A 4RH

A catalogue record for this book is available from the British Library.

Hardback ISBN: 1 85434 363 7
Paperback ISBN: 1 85434 364 5

Dewey Decimal Classification 937

Photographic credits: AKG London/Erich Lessing: p38, p51, p59; Ancient Art & Architecture Collection: p49;
British Musuem: p42; BM/The Bridgeman Art Library: p60; C M Dixon: p12, p25, p44; Elsevier Archive/
Atlas of the Roman World: p16; Michael Holford: p19, p28, p32, p36, p40, p48; Peter Clayton: p50;
Planet Earth Pictures: p4 (tr); Scala: p4 (bl), p24; Tony Stone/Jean Pragan: p60; Zefa: p46.

With thanks to the models: Sarah Abbott, Nadine Case, Francesca Collins, Tracy Ann Francis, Sammie-Jo Gold,
Matthew Harper, Aaron Haseley, Amanda Kwakye, Dean Newell, Jonathan Page, Davina Plummer,
Robin Richards, Sean Richardson, James Sayle, Jamie White, Daniel Wright, Jia Jia Wang and Ali Issaq
and to Wixs Lane School in Clapham, London.

Printed by Wing King Tong, Hong Kong

Paperback 2 4 6 8 10 9 7 5 3 1

◁ The **fasces** was a bundle of rods tied around an axe. It was an Etruscan symbol of power that was later used by the Romans.

THE ETRUSCANS were a powerful people. In the seventh century BC, Rome came under their influence and was ruled by a series of Etruscan kings. The Etruscans were good builders and they gave Rome its first large temples.

THE GREEKS were another important influence on the Romans. They founded cities around the coast of southern Italy. The Romans copied Greek buildings and sculptures, and were influenced by Greek legends and ideas.

ROMAN CIVILIZATION lasted for many centuries. To help make sense of it, we have divided it into different periods. Each period has been given a **symbol**, to show when information relates to that time. If there are no symbols, the information covers all periods.

The Republic refers to that period in Roman history when Rome was ruled by elected officials, and the Empire started to expand. By 27 BC the Republic had collapsed and was replaced by the rule of **emperors**. Under their rule, the Empire continued to expand. Later, the Empire was divided into two parts: the Eastern and Western Empires.

KEY FOR SYMBOLS

🦅 (eagle)   **Roman Republic** 509-27 BC

💮 (wreath)   **early imperial period** 27 BC-AD 284

☧ (Chi-Rho) **late imperial period** AD 284-476

THE MAKE IT WORK! way of looking at history is to ask questions about the past and to discover some of the answers by making copies of the things people made. However, you do not need to make everything in the book in order to understand the Roman way of life.

▽ This map shows how, over many centuries, the ancient Romans were influenced by different peoples.

EUROPE

ITALY

SARDINIA

North Africans control Sardinia and Sicily

■ Rome

Etruscans control Rome

SICILY

N. AFRICA

GREECE

Greeks settle in Sicily and southern Italy

Timeline

Rome was ruled by kings until 509 BC. After this time, the Romans set up a new form of government called the Republic. Instead of a king, the Romans were ruled by two officials called **consuls**, elected each year from among the leading **citizens**. This system lasted for almost 500 years. During this period, Rome grew from a small city to become the capital of a huge empire.

DURING THE REPUBLIC, as the Roman Empire grew, so did the size of its armies and the influence of the generals who commanded them. In the first century BC, there were bloody wars in which rival generals fought each other for power. Eventually, only one remained: Octavian. He became the first emperor of Rome and renamed himself Augustus. He called himself the 'first citizen', rather than 'emperor' and pretended that he had saved the Republic. But although consuls were still elected, real power lay with the emperor.

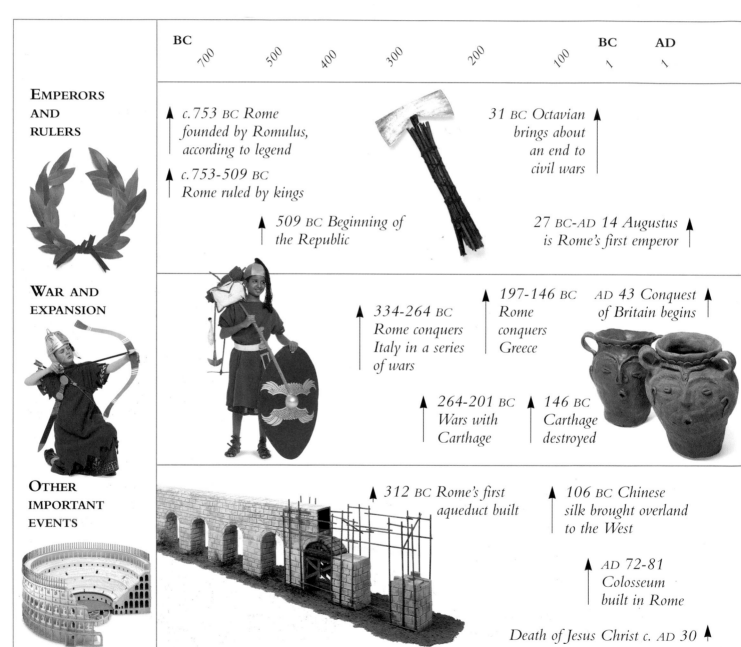

	BC						BC	AD
	700	500	400	300	200	100	1	1

EMPERORS AND RULERS

- *c.753 BC Rome founded by Romulus, according to legend*
- *c.753-509 BC Rome ruled by kings*
- *509 BC Beginning of the Republic*
- *31 BC Octavian brings about an end to civil wars*
- *27 BC-AD 14 Augustus is Rome's first emperor*

WAR AND EXPANSION

- *334-264 BC Rome conquers Italy in a series of wars*
- *264-201 BC Wars with Carthage*
- *197-146 BC Rome conquers Greece*
- *146 BC Carthage destroyed*
- *AD 43 Conquest of Britain begins*

OTHER IMPORTANT EVENTS

- *312 BC Rome's first aqueduct built*
- *106 BC Chinese silk brought overland to the West*
- *AD 72-81 Colosseum built in Rome*
- *Death of Jesus Christ c. AD 30*

THE FIRST EMPEROR, AUGUSTUS, was a successful ruler. His reign lasted for over 40 years and the Romans got used to being ruled by just one man. When Augustus died, his adopted son, Tiberius, became emperor after him. The Empire continued to grow until, in AD 117, it reached its greatest extent. The emperor needed people he could trust to help him rule the Empire, so he appointed governors to each of the **provinces**. Most of the army's time was spent defending the borders against foreign invaders.

THE HISTORY OF ROME is not just about emperors and wars. As time passed, many changes took place in the way that people lived. Through trade, they were introduced to new goods, such as Chinese silk. Their beliefs also changed as they came across foreign religions. The Syrians introduced them to the worship of the Sun; from Egypt they learned about the goddess **Isis**. But the religion that was to have the greatest effect was Christianity. In the fourth century AD, this became the official religion of the Empire.

AD

100   200   300   400

AD 284-305 Beginning of late imperial period – Empire is divided

AD 330 Constantine makes Constantinople capital of the Empire

AD 476 Romulus Augustulus, the last western emperor, is overthrown

AD 212 All free people within the Empire declared citizens by Emperor Caracalla

AD 324 Constantine reunites the Empire

AD 395 Empire is finally split into two halves

AD 117 Empire is at its largest

AD 410 Rome is captured and ransacked

AD 378 Goths defeat Romans at battle of Adrianople, killing the eastern emperor, Valens

AD 64 Great fire in Rome. Emperor Nero blames the Christians

AD 395 Christianity becomes official religion

AD 79 The volcano Vesuvius erupts, burying Pompeii

Eastern Empire survives until medieval times

AD 122 Emperor Hadrian orders building of wall across northern Britain

A conquering force

In the year AD 117, the Roman Empire reached its greatest size. It stretched 4,000 kilometres from east to west, 3,700 kilometres from north to south, and had a population of over 50 million people.

THE WESTERN half of the Empire was conquered as a result of rivalry between the Romans and the people of Carthage. The Carthaginians were a powerful seafaring people in North Africa who also controlled Sardinia, parts of Sicily and southern Spain. During a series of wars, Rome defeated Carthage and claimed its territory. The Romans later moved into northern Europe, conquering northern Spain, France, parts of Germany and Britain.

THE EAST mostly came under Roman control during the last two centuries BC. The Romans first went east to fight a people from northern Greece who were allied with Carthage. After defeating them, more wars of conquest followed. By 30 BC most of the lands around the Mediterranean were part of the Roman Empire. Roman rule put an end to fighting between rival states and brought peace.

▷ *This is a map of the Empire during the second century AD. Some important provinces are marked in capital letters. Provincial capitals, important cities and army bases are given with their Roman names. You could compare the names to those on a modern map of Europe.*

BRITANNIA

Londinium

Isca

Colonia Agrippina

GERMANIA

Mogontiacum

Calleva

GAUL

Legio

IBERIA

Massilia

Lugdunum

Toletum

Roma

Ostia

Emerita Augustus

ITALIA

Hispalis

Mediterranean Sea

Carthago

Thugga

MAURETANIA

AFRICA

KEY TO SYMBOLS

legionary base

provincial capital

important city

road

---- *provincial border*

TWO LANGUAGES held the Empire together. In the west, educated people learned to speak Latin; in the east, they spoke Greek. The Romans looked down on all other languages. Foreigners who could not speak Latin or Greek were called **barbarians**, because their speech sounded to Romans like a string of meaningless 'bar-bar' sounds.

ROMAN CITIZENSHIP was given to the most important people in the conquered lands. This meant that they were allowed to become Romans. Citizens had many rights denied to non-citizens. A male citizen could vote in local government, or stand for election. Becoming a citizen was like taking on a new identity: a citizen even had to take a Roman name and learn how to wear Roman clothes.

THE NUMBER OF ROMAN CITIZENS grew steadily over time. In 28 BC, there were four million: 80 years later, the figure had risen to six million. Finally in AD 212, the Emperor Caracalla allowed all free men and women, including ex-slaves, to become citizens.

Aquincum

Viminacium

Troesmia

Black Sea

Satala

ANATOLIA

Hadrianopolis

DALMATIA

Cyrrhus

Antiocha

Pompeii

Palmyra

Thessalonica

Ephesus

SYRIA

MACEDONIA

Legio

Mediterranean Sea

Alexandria

Cyrene

Aelia Capitolina

JUDEA

CYRENAICA

AEGYPTUS

Red Sea

From emperor to slave

The people of the Empire belonged to separate groups and classes, each with different rights. During the early imperial period, the most important distinction was between Roman citizens and non-citizens, or **provincials**. Citizens had more rights than provincials, and even dressed differently.

SLAVES were men, women and children who were owned as property and who were bought and sold in the market-place. Some were captured in wars, others were the children of slave parents. Household slaves could be secretaries, tutors, entertainers, cooks or servants. These slaves were far better off than those who worked on farms or down in the mines.

double pipes

▷ *A provincial farmer from northern Europe.*

▷ *A freedman could become a successful tradesman.*

△ *A household slave who is also a musician.*

ROMAN SLAVES who had been given their freedom were called **freedmen** and **freedwomen**. Many slaves saved up money and bought their freedom; others were freed by their owners as a reward for loyal service.

 PROVINCIALS, or non-citizens, had different degrees of wealth and status. Unlike slaves, they could serve in the army in special support, or 'auxiliary' units. After many years of service, **auxiliaries** and their families were usually given Roman citizenship. This was one way in which the number of citizens steadily increased.

trousers were worn in the cold north

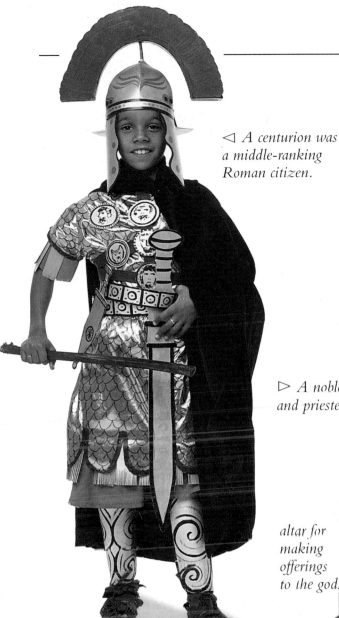

◁ *A centurion was a middle-ranking Roman citizen.*

WOMEN had fewer rights than men. They could not vote or follow careers in politics or law. Most wealthy Roman women looked after children and the home, and gave orders to slaves. However, women could own property and some ran their own businesses. Other women played important roles as priestesses in the temples (see page 35).

❨❩ ✳ **THE EMPEROR** had enormous power. He was the chief priest of the Roman religion and the overall commander of Rome's armies. He appointed governors to rule the different provinces of the Empire. Statues of him stood in every city and his face appeared on every coin.

laurel wreath

▷ *A noblewoman and priestess.*

purple **toga**

altar for making offerings to the gods

ROMAN CITIZENS were divided into different 'orders' or ranks, depending on their wealth and family background. At the top were the wealthy nobles who belonged to the order of **senators**. They were the generals, chief priests and governors of the most important provinces. Below them were **equestrians**, wealthy people who became civil servants, high-ranking officers or governors of smaller provinces. Lower still were ordinary citizens. They ranged from **centurions** and **legionaries**, to wealthy traders and poor farmers.

△ *The emperor was the most important person in Roman society.*

Togas and tunics

Roman men, women and children wore a simple tunic, made of wool or linen, with a belt around the waist. Some tunics had sleeves, like a T-shirt; others had armholes. It was the one item of clothing that everyone wore, rich and poor alike. Women's tunics were longer than men's, reaching to below the knees.

MALE ROMAN CITIZENS were supposed to wear a toga in public. The toga was a huge, semi-circular, woollen sheet that was wrapped around the body and arranged with folds. It took time and skill to put it on properly. Slaves and non-citizens wore the simple tunic, or *tunica*.

DIFFERENT COLOURED TOGAS were also a sign of status. Men standing for election wore a pure white toga. This has given us the word candidate, from the Latin word *candidus* (white). **Magistrates** and the young sons of wealthy families wore a *toga praetexta*, which was white with a purple border. The emperor wore a *toga picta*, which was purple with gold embroidery.

△ *This group of senators are all wearing togas. The Roman on the far right also holds the* fasces *symbol.*

⚘ ✳ **WOMEN** had a great variety of clothing. Some wore the *peplos* – a robe that fastened at the shoulders. Wealthy women wore clothes of brightly coloured Chinese silk and Indian cotton over their *tunica*, and decorated themselves with jewellery.

FOOTWEAR included various kinds of leather sandals. Slaves and citizens in warmer provinces wore simple sandals, like modern flip-flops. Soldiers wore stronger sandals with hobnails on the soles.

MAKE A PEPLOS

You will need: needle, thread, scissors, an old cotton sheet cut in half lengthwise, string, coloured wool, long cocktail sticks, thin wire, gold paint

1 Fold over a third of the material on each piece. You could hem the edges to prevent fraying. You will need to hold the material as shown above, up to your shoulders, in the final stage.

2 To make pins, twist the wire around the top of the cocktail sticks and tie a bow as above. Paint the pins gold.

3 For the belt, twist the string and long strands of coloured wool together as shown above. Knot both ends.

4 Ask a friend to help you put on the *peplos*. Push the pins through the folded fabric at the shoulders. Tie the belt at the waist and over the flaps of material.

MAKE A PAIR OF ROMAN SANDALS

You will need: brown felt or leather square, laces, pen, paper, scissors

1 If possible, enlarge the design above on a photocopier, so that it will fit your foot. Or, copy the design onto paper.

2 Cut out the design and draw around it on the fabric.

3 Turn the paper over and copy the design again, for your other foot. Then, cut out both shapes.

4 Stand on the centre of each piece of fabric. Use laces, or strips of the spare fabric, to lace up the loops in the sandal, as shown above.

PURPLE DYE was specially valued by the Romans. It came from a rare shellfish called the murex, found in parts of the Mediterranean.

WEAR A TOGA

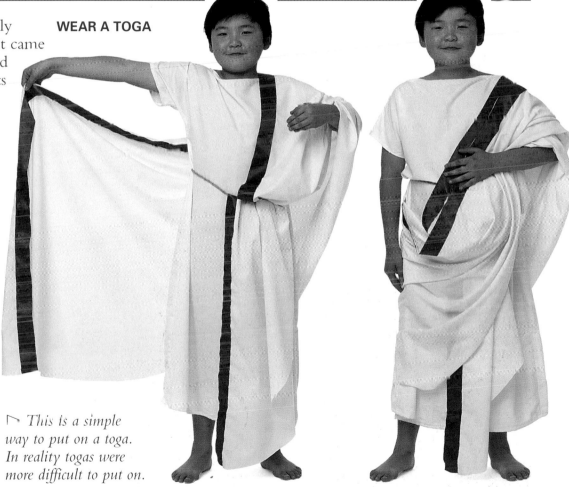

▷ *This is a simple way to put on a toga. In reality togas were more difficult to put on.*

You will need: semi-circular piece of fabric with a straight edge of 4 metres

1 Hold the straight edge of the fabric behind you. Drape half over your left arm. Tuck this section into your belt.

2 Pass the right half of the toga under your right arm and around the front. Tuck a little fold in your belt.

3 Now pass the rest of the fabric over your left shoulder.

Dressing to impress

Wealthy Romans went to great lengths to keep up with changing fashions. They started each day in front of a mirror, attended by slaves who dressed their hair, applied their make-up and perfume, and plucked out unwanted hair with tweezers.

{ } WOMEN'S HAIRSTYLES became more and more elaborate over time. They wore wigs and hairpieces curled with heated tongs and piled up high in rows of curls. Hairpins, made from bone or metal, held the curls in place. Some women wore wigs so that they could change the colour of their hair. Blond wigs were made with hair clipped from German slave girls, and black wigs were made with hair imported from India.

▷ *A wealthy or noble Roman woman spent a lot of time making her hair look beautiful.*

MEN WORE LAUREL WREATHS on their heads as a mark of rank. Victorious generals wore them on their return from successful campaigns, and Roman emperors wore them as crowns.

MAKE A LAUREL WREATH

You will need: fresh bay (laurel) leaves, or leaves made from green card, strips of green tissue paper, scissors, glue, plastic-coated wire, red ribbon

1 Shape the wire into a headband. Wind and glue strips of tissue paper around the band. Starting at one end, glue the leaves to the tissue paper as shown above right.

2 When you have reached half-way around the headband, start at the other end and glue on the rest of the leaves. Finally, snip the ends of the ribbon in a V-shape, and glue as shown right.

{ } WEARING MAKE-UP was important to noblewomen. They used paint made from chalk and white lead to whiten the face and forearms, and powdered ashes to blacken the eyebrows. Red ochre (from earth), or red wine leftovers were used as rouge for cheeks and lips. Women also used face packs made from damp bread, which they hoped would prevent wrinkles.

◁ *Many women wore beautiful metal bracelets shaped like coiling snakes.*

MAKE A ROMAN BROOCH

You will need: card, glue, safety pin, fine string, tape, paints, paintbrush

1 Draw two flower shapes on the card – one a little larger than the other. Draw four petal shapes, lots of little stamens and a small circle. Cut out the shapes carefully.

2 Glue bits of string around the petals and the circle. Glue lengths of string to the tips of the stamens.

3 Paint all the card shapes and pieces of string gold.

4 When dry, paint the insides of the petals different colours.

5 Glue the smaller flower on top of the larger one. Bend the edges inwards slightly. Glue the stamens onto the centre of the flower. Then glue on the petals and the circle as shown.

6 To wear your brooch, tape a safety pin onto the back, as shown above.

▽ *Brooches like these were used to fasten cloaks.*

▽ *The laurel-wreath crown was a symbol of military success and power.*

✿ ✳ **MEN'S HAIRSTYLES** were influenced by the emperor, whose portrait was engraved on coins (see page 51). Until the second century AD, men shaved their chins, or had them plucked with tweezers by a barber. This style changed when the Emperor Hadrian, who had an ugly scar on his chin, let his beard grow to hide it. Men all over the Empire followed his example.

Some men took just as much trouble over their appearance as women. This is how the historian Suetonius described the Emperor Otho: 'He was as fussy about his appearance as a woman. His entire body had been plucked of hair and a well-made wig covered his practically bald head… He used a poultice of moist bread to slow down the growth of his beard.'

Life in the city

Many Romans lived in the large cities of the Empire. These cities were often built near rivers or close to the sea, because it was much easier to move heavy goods by water than by road. Cities were the main trading centres. There was a constant movement of wagons, pack animals and merchant ships arriving and departing.

ROMAN CITIES were often built on a grid system. Blocks of buildings called **insulae** were divided by straight streets. Each *insula* was packed with houses, shops and workshops. To save space, these buildings often joined onto each other, like a row of terraced houses.

△ *This is an aerial photograph of the Roman town of Timgad in Algeria. The grid system can be seen clearly.*

▽ *This is a model of a typical Roman town. Most towns and cities had the same key buildings.*

FRESH WATER was brought into the city by an **aqueduct**. A lot of water was needed for drinking and for the public baths, where Romans went to relax. Many cities also had sewers, and public toilets flushed by water.

split aqueduct carries water into covered reservoirs

market-place   *public baths*

AT THE HEART OF EVERY ROMAN CITY was the **forum**. This was a large open area, used as a market and a public meeting place. Along one side there was a long hall called a *basilica*. This was the law court and the place where merchants and wealthy Romans met to do business.

A smaller building nearby, the *curia*, was where the local council met. The council was responsible for putting on public entertainment, keeping law and order, raising taxes and looking after the roads, public buildings and the water supply.

TEMPLES for worshipping the most important gods and the Roman emperor were also built in the forum. Temples to local gods were scattered across the town. Wealthy Romans helped to pay for building temples, and in return had their names carved on them.

PUBLIC ENTERTAINMENT was an important part of city life. There were theatres for plays, and **amphitheatres** where fights between **gladiators** were held (see pages 38-39). Some of the bigger cities even had a racecourse for chariot racing.

theatre　　city gates　　　　amphitheatre　　basilica　*forum*　　　temple　　　insula

curia

POMPEII is a town in Italy that was buried under ash when the volcano Vesuvius erupted violently in AD 79. Over the past 200 years, the houses and shops of Pompeii have been slowly uncovered. As a result, we have a picture of a whole Roman town as it was on an August day nearly 2,000 years ago.

terracotta roof

wooden rafters

balcony

workshop where felt was made

△ *The poorer people of Pompeii and other Roman cities, lived above or behind shops in streets like this.*

many people bought bread in public bakeries

THE STREETS of Pompeii were lined with a variety of shops and bars. These were often run by freedmen who had their own slaves working for them. Each shop had a large, open front that was closed up with wooden shutters at night. There was a counter at the front where goods were displayed to customers in the street. Taverns had stone counters with jars set into them for snacks and hot drinks.

△ *In this excavated street in Pompeii you can see the deep ruts in the road made by cart wheels.*

THE PAVEMENTS IN POMPEII, like those of many Roman cities, were raised above the level of the road. This prevented ox-carts from knocking over pedestrians. The road sloped slightly so that rainwater and sewage ran into the gutters. Stepping-stones were laid across the road to allow people to cross without getting their sandals dirty, and also to slow down the carts.

MOST PEOPLE IN THE EMPIRE were poor, although those who were in charge were very rich. In the larger cities, the poor lived in rented rooms in blocks of flats or apartments. In smaller towns, rich and poor alike lived in the *insulae*, or blocks of housing. A rich family might own a large part of the *insula*, whereas a poor family rented perhaps only one or two rooms.

Inside the homes, furniture was very simple. The poet Martial described a typical room: 'There was a little three-legged bed and a two-legged table, with a lamp and a bucket… The neck of an **amphora** held back a little cooker covered in green rust.' Most homes did not have bathrooms. Instead, people used chamber pots which they emptied out of their windows onto the street below.

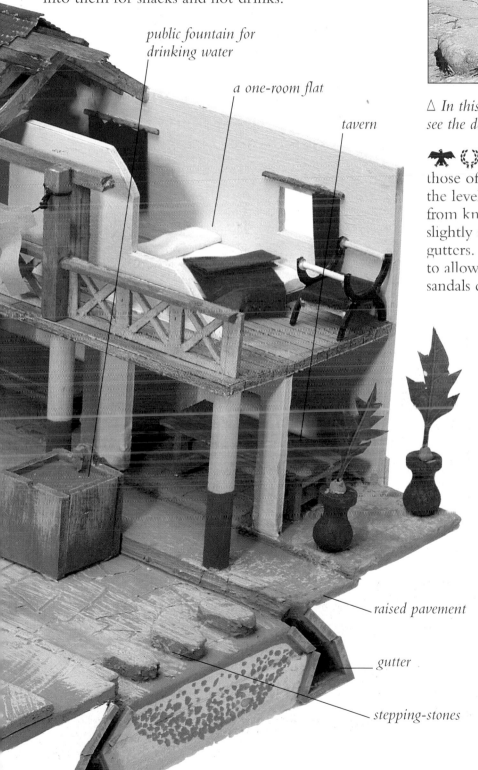

public fountain for drinking water

a one-room flat

tavern

raised pavement

gutter

stepping-stones

WEALTHY ROMANS lived in very different conditions from the poor. From the outside, the houses of wealthy Romans looked very plain. Because of the risk of burglary, most houses had only a few windows. Rooms were arranged around courtyards and gardens, and openings in the roof let in the maximum amount of light.

△ In the evenings, homes were lit with pottery lamps. The lamps burned oil made from olives, nuts or fish.

THE FIRST ROOM people entered in a Roman house was called the *atrium*. It was a cross between an entrance hall and a courtyard. It had a high ceiling with a skylight in the middle. Below this, in the centre of the *atrium*, was an ornamental pool to collect rainwater.

THE DINING ROOM was called a *triclinium*, meaning 'three couches'. The houses of the rich sometimes had two *triclinia*; a sheltered one for the winter, and one with a view of the garden for the summer.

THE RECEPTION ROOM was the *tablinum*. This was a cross between a living room and an office where guests were received. Important papers and valuables were kept there, safely locked in a strongbox.

A ROMAN HOUSE was often a crowded place. There were household slaves running errands, children playing with toys, and older women spinning wool together (see pages 30–31). There was also a stream of daily visitors or **clients** who came to ask advice and favours from their 'patron' – the head of the house. These were generally people who were less well off. For a wealthy Roman, the day began with a visit from his clients. The more important a Roman was, the greater the number of clients who visited him.

▷ *A wealthy Roman might have lived in a town house like this.*

bedroom
(above tablinum)

peristyle
garden (see
page 23)

BEDROOMS were often alongside the *atrium*. Apart from the bed, there was little furniture – perhaps a chair and a table, and a pottery chamber pot kept underneath the bed.

CLIENTS were expected to arrive in a clean toga, and to call their patron 'my lord'. They would wait in the *atrium* until a slave summoned them to the *tablinum*, where the patron would receive them.

These wealthy patrons were themselves the clients of still richer men. After they had greeted their clients, they might have to visit their own patron. The only man who did not have a patron was the emperor.

rooms were decorated with **frescoes** *and* **mosaics** *(see pages 24-25)*

rooms at the front were rented to tradesmen

triclinium

atrium with skylight and pool for rainwater

kitchen

Gardens, mosaics and frescoes

Wealthy Romans loved their gardens. They were neatly laid out with rows of clipped hedges and paths, and filled with fountains, pools and statues. A garden was a place to relax on a sunny day, to read or write, or just do nothing.

▷ *The gardens of a Roman town house or country villa may have been circular, like this one, or rectangular.*

MANY GARDENS have been discovered at Pompeii. Although the plants there disappeared long ago, their roots have left spaces in the soil. Archaeologists make plaster casts of these spaces to find out what kinds of trees and bushes were planted there.

hedges trimmed to look like birds

lemon tree

small bust of a forest spirit

fountain

FOUNTAINS and ornamental pools were carved from marble. Pliny the Younger, a writer, described the fountains of his garden: 'A fountain plays in a marble basin, watering the plane trees round it and the ground beneath them with its light spray… Another has a bowl surrounded by tiny jets which make a lovely murmuring sound.'

STATUES of gods and fighting animals were popular garden ornaments. The 'House of Stags' in Herculaneum in southern Italy, is named after two sculptures of stags being attacked by dogs. There were also statues of forest spirits such as satyrs, which were young men with the legs, ears and horns of goats.

△ Oscilla *were decorated with reliefs of gods and satyrs.*

THE PERISTYLE was a type of garden surrounded by roofed columns that gave shade. White marble or terracotta discs called *oscilla* were hung between the columns for decoration. They flashed like tiny mirrors as they caught the sun.

SLAVES who were skilled gardeners looked after the garden. They clipped bushes into the shape of animals, birds and gods. The wealthiest Romans also liked to have fish tanks in their gardens, filled with fish, eels and other seafood. They provided a fresh supply for the dinner table! Exotic birds were also popular. Peacocks were imported from India and were thought to be the sacred bird of the goddess Juno.

GARDEN WALLS were sometimes painted with pictures of trees, birds and flowers to make the gardens look bigger. If a house had no real garden, Romans painted garden scenes on a wall, to give the impression of one. Some of these still survive today. They show us what kind of plants the Romans liked to grow.

△ *This mosaic from Pompeii shows a scene from the banks of the River Nile in Egypt. The Romans hunted many of these animals and brought them back to Rome for the games (see pages 38-39).*

THE TOWN HOUSES AND COUNTRY VILLAS of wealthy Romans were full of colour. The walls of important rooms, such as the *triclinium* and *tablinum*, were covered with bright paintings called frescoes. The floors were decorated with mosaics – pictures made from thousands of tiny coloured tiles and pieces of glass.

MOSAICS were fashionable throughout the Empire. The Romans used the technique, developed by the Greeks, of making black and white patterned floors with pebbles. Later, coloured floors became popular. By cutting stones, glass, tiles and shells into little pieces known as *tesserae*, the Romans could make mosaics as detailed as paintings. There were scenes from everyday life, flowers, and different figures such as the gods, gladiators and actors. One house in Pompeii had a mosaic of a snarling dog in the doorway, with the words *'cave canem'*, 'beware of the dog', written into the mosaic.

MAKE A MOSAIC

You will need: paper, felt-tip pens, scissors, self-hardening clay, paints, paintbrush, stiff card, rolling pin, tile adhesive, sponge or stiff brush, varnish (optional)

1 Draw a fish or another animal. Then cut a piece of stiff card, large enough to cover the whole design.

2 Draw your design on a piece of paper and choose the colours you would like to use.

3 Roll out the clay with the rolling pin until it is about 3 mm thick.

4 Use a pair of scissors to mark the clay into small squares, as shown above right.

5 Cut the squares to make small tiles, or *tesserae*. Leave them to dry out.

6 Paint them in your chosen colours.

7 To create a more textured effect, you could dip a sponge in the paint and dab it gently onto the tiles. Or you could flick paint onto them, using a stiff brush.

FRESCOES were painted on a freshly plastered wall that was still damp. The colour soaked into the plaster and became fixed as it dried. The finished wall was given a protective coat of melted wax mixed with a little oil. Finally, the surface was polished to give it a glossy appearance.

THE FIRST PAINTERS only had a few colours to work with: black from soot, white from chalk, and red and yellow ochre from earth. As the Empire grew, more colours became available. The Egyptians showed the Romans how to make a rich shade of blue from copper. Vermilion, a bright scarlet, came from a mineral called cinnabar which was mined in Spain. Even more exotic and expensive colours were brought by sea from India. You could tell how wealthy Romans were simply by looking at the colours on the walls of their houses.

STYLES OF PAINTING came and went. Until about 80 BC, walls were painted to look as if they were made of coloured marble. Then, architectural scenes with columns and statues became popular. The aim was to make a room look bigger than it really was.

△ This fresco was discovered on the wall of a town house in Pompeii. The young woman is holding a writing tablet in one hand and a **stylus** in the other (see page 33).

△ Mosaics of sea creatures were sometimes used to decorate triclinium floors.

8 Cover the stiff card with a layer of tile adhesive. Press the tiles into the adhesive, following your paper design. Begin with the centre tiles and work outwards until the design is complete.

9 Leave the mosaic to dry. You could varnish it later.

Food and feasting

The staple food of most Romans was a type of stew, made from wheat, barley, beans or lentils. However, rich Romans had a more varied diet. They ate food grown on their own farms, and more expensive dishes imported from all over the Empire.

COOKING was a luxury for most people who lived in cities. Because of the risk of fire in their wooden apartments, the poor bought their meals from stalls in the street instead of cooking. Wealthy Romans had their own kitchens, and slaves who cooked for them.

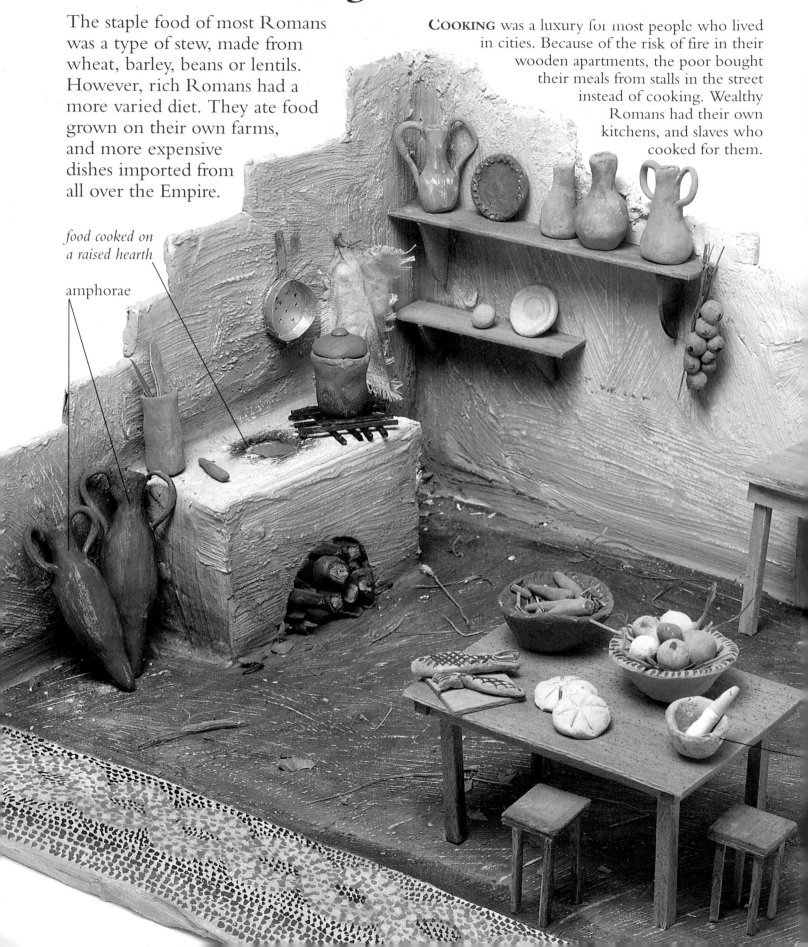

food cooked on a raised hearth

amphorae

MAKE A HONEY OMELETTE

You will need: five eggs, ground pepper, 10 g butter, 75 ml milk, 5 ml honey, 25 g almonds, dash of anchovy essence or soy sauce

1 Whisk the eggs in a bowl. Then add the honey, pepper and milk.

2 Ask an adult to put the almonds on a baking tray and bake them in a hot oven 165° C (325° F) for 20 mins.

3 When cool, ask an adult to chop the nuts with a sharp knife. Now add them to the egg mixture.

4 Stir the anchovy essence or soy sauce into the egg mixture.

5 Melt the butter in a frying pan and pour in the egg mixture. Cook until the omelette is firm, turning once.

BRICK OVENS were used for baking and roasting. A fire was lit inside, heating the bricks. When the fire died, the ashes were raked out and bread or meat was pushed in. The entrance was covered and food cooked by the heat of the bricks.

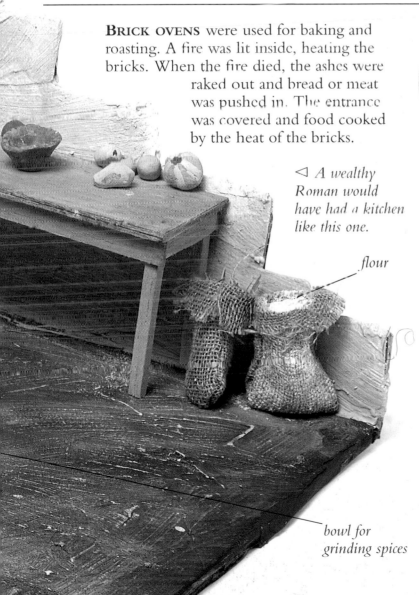

◁ *A wealthy Roman would have had a kitchen like this one.*

flour

bowl for grinding spices

POTTERY JARS, or *amphorae*, leaned against the kitchen walls. They held the most commonly used ingredients – olive oil, vinegar, wine and fish sauce.

THE MOST POPULAR FOOD FLAVOURING was a spicy fish sauce called *garum*. It was made from the blood and internal parts of mackerel, an oily type of fish. The fish parts were salted, mixed with vinegar and herbs, and left in the sun until they turned into liquid. *Garum* had a powerful flavour. Only a tiny amount was needed to flavour a dish.

THE ROMANS COOKED their food rather differently to how we cook today. They used honey to sweeten food, because they did not have sugar. They also loved pepper, which came from India. They even sprinkled it on desserts and mixed it with wine.

MAKE GRAPE PUNCH

3 Ask an adult to help you heat the ingredients. Stir them continuously over a low heat for half an hour.

4 Leave to cool before serving.

You will need: four tablespoons of honey, crushed bay leaf, two dates, one litre white grape juice, pinch of: cinnamon, ground pepper, saffron and lemon for flavour and decoration

1 Chop the dates finely. Discard the stones.

2 Place all the ingredients in a saucepan.

ENTERTAINING generally took place in the evening, when wealthy Romans invited guests to dinner. They ate in the *triclinium*, or dining room, stretched out on three couches.

◁ *The Romans made beautiful glassware which they used when they entertained.*

EACH COUCH could seat three people, so the perfect number of guests at a dinner party was nine. The couches were arranged to make three sides of a square, with the fourth side left open for the slaves who brought the dishes.

▷ *The Romans served this spiced punch cold before a meal, or warm if served during a meal.*

DORMICE were a popular dish. They were kept inside pottery jars and fattened until they were ready to cook. Then they were served sprinkled with honey and poppy seeds!

mosaics of food scraps

THE PLACE OF HONOUR was on the right-hand side of the host who lay in the centre of the middle couch. The guests propped themselves up on their elbows and ate with their fingers. Between courses they washed their hands in finger bowls and dried them with napkins. Guests often brought their own napkins, so that they could take away any of the delicious food they had been unable to finish.

ROMANS SHOWED OFF THEIR WEALTH by serving food brought from all the corners of the Empire. Certain provinces were famous for particular delicacies. Libya, for example, was the place to find truffles, while Syria was known for its delicious pears.

burning lamps for light

▽ *A Roman dinner party in the* triclinium.

○ **UNUSUAL DISHES** were especially impressive. The Emperor Vitellius, famous for his love of food, served some of the most expensive meals in history. One of his dishes, called 'Shield of Minerva', was described by the historian Suetonius: 'The recipe called for pike-livers, pheasant-brains, peacock-brains, flamingo-tongues, and lamprey-eggs [an eel-like fish]; and the ingredients, collected in every corner of the Empire… were brought to Rome in naval *triremes* [warships].'

THROUGHOUT THE MEAL, slaves who were musicians, storytellers and jugglers would entertain the guests. The type of entertainment depended on the tastes of the host. He might want to read legal speeches or extracts from his poetry. Another host might only be interested in belly-dancing!

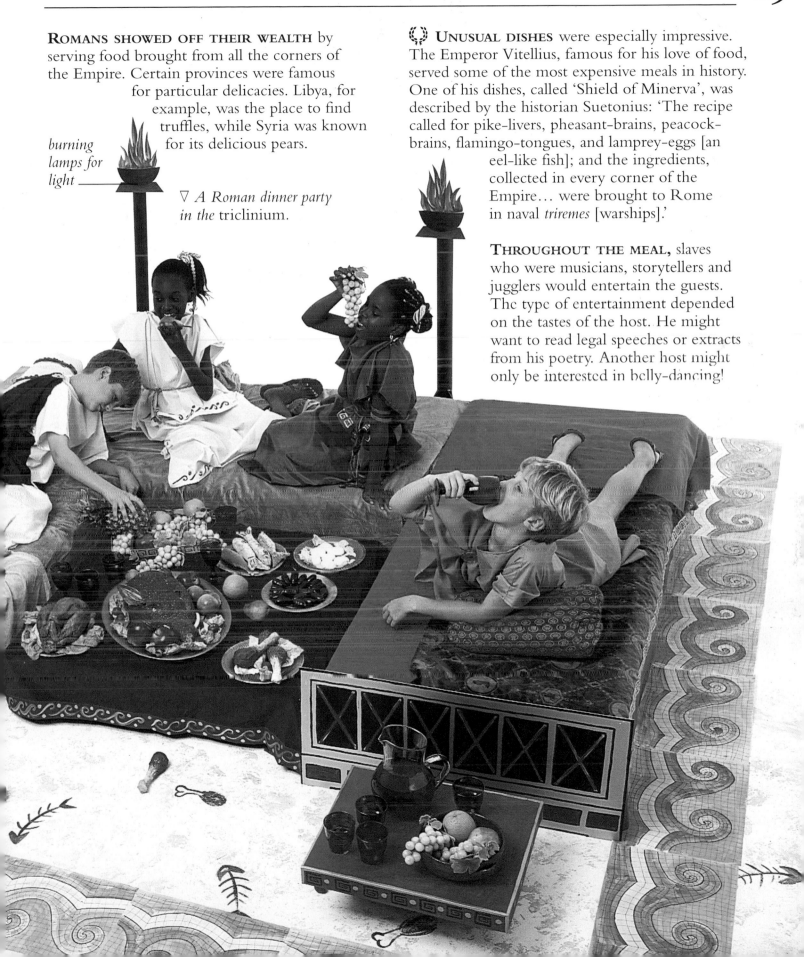

Family life

The word 'family' is Roman and comes from the Latin word *familia*. In Roman times, a family meant the household, which included slaves, freedmen and freedwomen.

POORER ROMANS were rarely educated. Unlike the wealthy, they did not write books and could not afford carved tombstones for their graves. Most of what we know about the daily lives of Romans comes from these sources. Because the rich were generally only interested in their own lives, not much is known about poorer Romans.

▷ *Young children played with terracotta rattles shaped like animals. This jewel-studded pig probably belonged to a child with wealthy parents.*

charm, or bulla – *a young boy's pendant*

family shrine

THE FAMILY HEAD was the father. He was known as the **pater familias**. He had total power over all family members and had the right to sell them into slavery, or even to kill them. Sons only became the *pater familias* of their families when their fathers died.

HOUSEHOLD GODS were thought to watch over every family. The head of the house was protected by a guardian spirit called his *Genius*, while his wife's guardian spirit was called her *Juno*. The *Penates* looked after the food cupboards, and the *Lares* protected the home. Small statues of these gods were kept in a household **shrine** and the family made offerings to them.

◁ *A boy offers a tuft of hair to the gods.*

CHILDREN made their own offerings to the household gods. When girls became engaged to be married, they left their toy dolls at the shrine as a sign that they were grown-up. When boys were first shaved by the barber, they offered some of the hair to the gods, to show that they had become men.

MAKE A ROMAN TOY DOLL

You will need: self-hardening clay, needle, string, paints, paintbrush

1 Model the clay into the parts of a doll: two arms, two legs, a body and head, as shown above right. At the base of the body, make two indents for the legs.

2 With the needle, make holes in the top of the arms and legs, through the base of the body, and right through the chest. The holes must be large enough for the string to be threaded through.

3 Leave the clay parts to dry.

4 Paint your doll as shown. Add a pattern around her neck, waist and hair for decoration. Leave to dry.

5 Thread string through the holes in the chest and arms. Knot the ends to secure. Do the same with the legs.

▷ *Roman children played with spinning tops, carved wooden animals, hoops and dolls like this one.*

🦅 🏛 **MARRIAGE** had a dramatic effect on the lives of Roman women. In early times, when a young girl married, she had to leave her own *familia* and join her husband's. This meant that she had to live by the rules of a new *pater familias*. But by the end of the Republic, the Romans had invented a new system of marriage in which a wife legally remained part of her own *familia*. This gave her more freedom. She kept control of her own property and if her husband divorced her, he had to return anything belonging to her.

DIVORCE was common, especially among wealthy Romans. A husband could divorce his wife if the marriage was childless, or if he wanted to marry someone else. But wives did not have the right to divorce their husbands.

WIVES were responsible for running the household, giving orders to slaves and looking after the children. They also spent a lot of time spinning thread from wool to make clothes. In marriage ceremonies, a bride often carried a spindle for hand-spinning as a symbol of her duties as a wife.

Education and trades

Life for the sons and daughters of wealthy Romans was very different to the lives of poor children. Children of the wealthy were educated at home or at school, whereas poorer children went out to learn a trade.

POOR CHILDREN did not go to school. From an early age, they were expected to help their parents at work. A young boy of eight or nine years would either follow in his father's footsteps, or work as an apprentice in the trade of a family friend. To begin with, child workers were usually given the most unpleasant tasks, but by watching and helping, boys learned the skills of blacksmiths, bakers, launderers and goldsmiths. Girls stayed with their mothers and helped in the shop, the workshop, or the kitchen.

▷ *This is a Roman inkpot and pen from the first century* AD.

RICH CHILDREN began their education at home, where they were taught by a well-educated slave called a *pedagogue*. At the age of 11, some boys and girls went to a school run by a *grammaticus*, or grammar teacher, to study literature. They learned to speak Greek and memorized Greek and Latin poetry, taking turns to recite it. Roman noblemen and women loved quoting poetry in their conversations and letters.

PUBLIC SPEAKING was considered to be essential for all young men wishing to become politicians or lawyers. A tutor called a *rhetor* taught pupils how to arrange an argument in a logical way and how to speak persuasively. Pupils practised these skills by imagining they were taking part in law cases, either defending or accusing.

◁ *In Pompeii, young boys were employed in laundries to clean cloth in large vats, by treading it with their feet.*

MAKE A WRITING TABLET

You will need: balsa wood, red and green Plasticine, craft knife, ruler, glue, string, paint, bradawl, twig

1 For both frames cut a flat piece of wood 18 cm x 14 cm, four thick strips of wood: two measuring 18 cm x 1 cm, and two measuring 14 cm x 1 cm. Glue together as shown above right.

2 Paint the frames a rich, woody colour. With the bradawl, make two holes in one side of each frame. Thread string through the holes and tie the frames together.

3 Make seals to decorate. Cut three 20 cm lengths of string. Press the string into three red Plasticine discs. Glue to the back of the tablet.

4 Roll out two flat pieces of green Plasticine and glue inside each frame as shown.

5 To make a *stylus*, ask an adult to help you sharpen the end of a twig. Use it to write on the tablet. Smooth over the Plasticine to use again.

ROMAN NUMERALS

1	I	7	VII	40	XL
2	II	8	VIII	50	L
3	III	9	IX	60	LX
4	IV	10	X	90	XC
5	V	20	XX	100	C
6	VI	30	XXX	500	D
				1,000	M

▷ *A noblewoman reads a letter written on a wax writing tablet.*

ROMANS used letters to stand for numbers, and they are still used today on clocks and watches. Each letter had a different value and could be combined with other letters to make bigger numbers. They used I for 1, X for 10 and C for 100, so for example 1,326 was shown as MCCCXXVI. This made it quite tricky to do calculations with large numbers, especially multiplication and long division.

PUPILS wrote on thin sheets of wood using pens made from reeds or brass. They also wrote on beeswax tablets using a pen called a *stylus* to scratch letters into the tablet. One end of the *stylus* was flat, so that the wax could be smoothed over and reused.

IN SOME ROMAN TOWNS walls were covered with advertisements, so it is likely that many of the poor could read. Despite the lack of formal teaching, many poorer Romans learned to read and write a little – enough to sign their names and write a few simple documents.

Gods of the Empire

The Romans believed in many gods and goddesses who were thought to watch over different aspects of their lives. From very early times the Romans adopted Greek myths, linking the legends of the Greek gods with their own. They told the same stories about Jupiter that the Greeks told of their god, Zeus.

THE MOST IMPORTANT GODS were Jupiter, ruler of gods and men, and king of heaven; his wife Juno, queen of heaven and goddess of women and marriage; and Jupiter's daughter Minerva, goddess of wisdom and art. Together, they shared the Temple of Jupiter Capitolinus in Rome. Temples were places to worship statues of the gods. They were also places to leave valuables for safe-keeping, like banks today. It was thought that thieves would not dare to rob the house of a god.

▽ *Musicians herald the arrival of the procession.*

long, curved horn called a cornu

double pipes

▽ *The* victimarius *(sacrificing priest) carries an axe.*

a sheep is led to the altar as an offering to the gods

RELIGIOUS CEREMONIES were conducted by a priest or priestess, in front of the temple building. Processions of people brought gifts as offerings to a particular god. In return they hoped to win the god's favour. Bulls, sheep and pigs were decorated with flowers and led to the temple. The priest or priestess sacrificed the animal on an altar in front of the temple, and then burned some of the meat. The rising smoke was supposed to carry the offering up to the god.

TELLING THE FUTURE was an important part of religion. The Romans believed that the gods sent messages to warn of coming disasters, or as a sign of good luck. There were different ways of reading these messages. **Augurs** were priests who told the future by studying birds. **Haruspices** were men who examined the inner organs of a sacrificed animal to find out if the god had accepted the offering.

▽ *On festival days processions of people made their way to the temple and made sacrifices to the gods.*

◁ *A **standard bearer** leads the procession.*

sacrifices are made on the altar

◁ *The priestess stands behind the altar, in front of the temple.*

(◌) ✳ **ROMAN EMPERORS** had temples built in their own honour where people could make offerings to their statues. Few people believed that the emperors really were gods, but they had to honour them as gods because it was a way of showing loyalty and respect. To refuse to do so was considered treason.

△ *This statue depicts Mithras slaying a legendary bull. The bull's blood was believed to be the source of all life.*

⚜ **AS THE EMPIRE EXPANDED,** the Romans came into contact with people who worshipped different gods. Some of these foreign gods were just like their own. Other gods, like **Mithras** and Isis, seemed very different, partly because they offered the promise of life after death.

⚜ **THE CULTS OF MITHRAS AND ISIS** were spread throughout the Empire by merchants, traders, soldiers and slaves. These gods were worshipped at secret ceremonies, unlike Roman gods who were worshipped in public. Mithras was the god of light from Persia (ancient Iran). He was worshipped by men who met by torchlight in underground rooms.

Isis was an Egyptian mother goddess and the special protector of seafarers. Followers of Isis were persecuted until Emperor Caligula built a temple to her and allowed people freedom of worship.

MAKE A VOTIVE OFFERING

5 Coil pieces of wire into rings. Make a hole at the top and bottom of the sweet shape and thread the rings through.

6 Make a hole in the leg shape and attach to the bottom ring. Tie the ribbon to the top ring.

You will need: thin card, strips of newspaper, flour, water, salt, wire, large needle, ribbon, bronze paint, paintbrush

1 Draw a leg or hand and 'sweet' shape on the card as shown, then cut them out.

2 Make a runny paste from flour and water. Add a pinch of salt. Cover the card with a few layers of newspaper strips dipped in the paste. Leave to dry.

3 Paint the card shapes bronze.

4 You could write your name in Roman capital letters with a needle as shown right.

△ *Votive offerings were left at temples in the hope of a cure for a specific ailment.*

⚜ **VOTIVES,** or dedicated offerings, were used in temples throughout the Empire. Romans believed that the gods had the power to cause and cure illness, so people who were sick went to the temple to pray. As an offering to the gods, they left a small model of the part of the body that needed healing, with a few words inscribed on it.

⚜ **SOME RELIGIOUS PRACTICES** are shrouded in mystery. Face pots, some containing ashes of the dead, have been found at Roman sites in Britain and Germany. They were discovered in graves, under buildings and in streams. No one knows what the faces mean: they may represent a dead person, a god or a mask.

⚜ ☧ **MAKE A FACE POT**

You will need: self-hardening clay, poster paints, paintbrush

1 Take a lump of clay and roll it out into several long sausage shapes. Coil a length of clay into a round base shape as shown above.

2 Carefully join on another coil of clay and build up your pot in this way. Use your thumbs to smooth the outside of the pot and merge the coils.

3 Make little clay petal shapes for the rim of the pot. Then make a mouth, eyes, eyebrows, nose and ears.

4 Carefully add the details to the pot and smooth the joins. Leave the pot to dry completely. Then paint it brown.

⚜ **CHRISTIANITY** spread from Palestine in the Eastern Empire during the first century AD. Like Mithras and Isis, Christ was seen as a god who promised eternal life. Unlike those gods however, his religion was open to everyone, including slaves and the poor. At first, Rome's rulers tried to stamp out this new religion because Christians refused to pay respect to the Roman gods, or worship the emperor.

☧ **ATTITUDES TO CHRISTIANITY CHANGED** when the Emperor Constantine came to power. He became a Christian, and in AD 313 he gave Christians the freedom of worship and encouraged Romans to convert.

△ Face pots, or funerary urns, were used in burial rituals.

At the games

The Romans had very bloodthirsty tastes in entertainment. They loved watching people and animals killing each other in the amphitheatre. There were many amphitheatres in the Empire, but the greatest was the Colosseum in Rome.

⟨⟩ **THE COLOSSEUM** in Rome opened in AD 80 and held up to 50,000 people. The games usually began with bloody battles between wild beasts. Then the gladiatorial contests followed. To celebrate the opening of the Colosseum, 5,000 animals were slaughtered on the first day.

▽ *The Colosseum in Rome.*

△ *Romans hunting animals in North Africa for the games.*

DURING THE FIRST HALF OF THE GAMES, wild animals, such as rhinoceros, lions, elephants and bulls were pitted against gladiators, and each other, or let loose on criminals.

for shade, an awning was tied to masts

the arena

supporting arches

underground chambers

statues of gods and emperors

arched entrance for spectators

entrance for senators and emperors

GLADIATORS were usually slaves or criminals, although some freedmen also earned their living this way. A gladiator's life was short and hard; the majority survived only a few fights.

SUCCESSFUL GLADIATORS were treated rather like the film stars of today. They were well-trained champions who were taught combat techniques at special schools. There were different types of gladiator: the *retiarius* was armed as a fisherman, with a net and a trident – he was often pitted against a *murmillo*, the fishman. Each type of gladiator had its own group of devoted fans.

A CONTEST LASTED until one gladiator was killed or badly wounded. The wounded man threw away his weapons and begged for mercy. The crowd would shout out a verdict. If the gladiator had fought well, the emperor would give a 'thumbs-up' sign and spare his life. If he had not fought well, the emperor gave the 'thumbs-down' sign. Then, the victorious gladiator would kill the loser. An attendant dressed as a demon clubbed the loser on the head and dragged his body out through the 'gate of death'.

▽ *A* retiarius *gladiator (right) defeats a* murmillo.

helmet

the gladiator begs for mercy by raising the forefinger of his left hand

arm shield

trident

gladiator's armour deliberately left vital organs, such as the heart, unprotected

greaves, or shin guards

sword

net with lead weights

shield

CHARIOT RACING was the most popular entertainment in the larger cities of the Empire. The Romans may have taken the sport from the Greeks who had been racing horses for over a thousand years.

RACES TOOK PLACE on a long track called a **circus**. The biggest of all, Rome's Circus Maximus, could hold 250,000 spectators. The circus was a place to meet friends, to gamble on the horses and to enjoy a dangerous and spectacular show.

▷ *Chariots were made from lightweight pieces of wood, lashed together with thongs. This bronze statue was once a two-horse chariot.*

▽ *Watching chariot racing at the Circus Maximus in Rome was a favourite pastime for many Romans.*

the emperor sat in the imperial box with his family and friends

the president started the races here

starting gates

arcades where food sellers and fortune tellers set up their stalls

turning point

THERE WERE FOUR TEAMS – the Whites, Reds, Blues and the Greens. Each team had its own horses, riders and stables, staffed with trainers, vets and slaves. Like football fans of today, race-goers supported one particular team. They gambled money on their team and wore its colours. The Blues and the Greens had the most supporters. Their rival fans hated each other so much that the races sometimes ended in riots.

THE RACETRACK was the only public place where men and women could sit together. According to the poet Ovid, the circus was a good place to find a girlfriend: 'Sit as close as you like; no one will stop you at all. In fact, you have to sit close – that's one of the rules at the racetrack... Ask her, "Whose colours are those?" – that's good for an opening. Put your bet down, fast, on whatever she plays... Girls, as everyone knows, adore these little attentions.'

THE PRESIDENT OF THE RACES sat at one end of the circus and it was his responsibility to get the race underway. At the blast of a trumpet, he stood up and held out a white napkin, which he dropped onto the track. At this signal, the starting gates flew open and the chariots came racing out.

The starting gates were situated at one end of the circus. Two or four chariots raced seven times around a long, narrow structure called a *spina* which had turning points at each end. The race finished opposite the judges' boxes about half-way along one side.

THE MOST DANGEROUS MOMENT was turning the chariots at the end of the track. If they were too close to the turning posts, they might crash into each other, or overturn. If they were too far away, the charioteers could lose their position.

CHARIOTEERS were mostly slaves. If they won races they could buy their freedom and grow very rich. The teams paid their stars huge salaries to stop them from joining a rival team. The fans admired their skill and courage so much that they kept busts and portraits of the charioteers in their homes. However, many charioteers died young, crushed under the hooves of the galloping horses.

spectators' seats

charioteers

triumphal arch where the chariots entered the circus in a procession

obelisk of Pharaoh Ramses II, brought from Egypt by the Emperor Augustus

spina

THE CENTRAL 'BACKBONE', or *spina*, of the circus, was decorated with statues of the gods and goddesses who were thought to watch over sport. There were also seven large wooden eggs and seven bronze dolphins on the *spina*. At the end of every lap, an egg was removed and a dolphin was reversed to show how many laps remained. Each end of the *spina* was marked by three tall posts.

THE BEST HORSES were also treated like stars. The Emperor Caligula had a favourite horse called *Incitatus* (Speedy) which raced for the Greens. He went to great lengths to keep his horse happy. On the day before a race, troops surrounded the stable, making sure that no-one made any loud noises that might disturb *Incitatus*. Caligula even gave the horse a house complete with furniture and slaves!

Romans relaxing

frigidarium   tepidarium   *furnace*   laconicum *or* caldarium   natatio

Every Roman town had at least one large public bath house. This was a place where people could go to wash the dust off, to exercise, or just to relax. Men and women visited the bath house separately, either at different times or to different areas. It cost very little to go to the baths, so only the poorest people could not afford to visit them. Many Romans went every day.

▷ *Oils were kept in the small pot, and the long, curved* **strigil** *was used for scraping off the oil and dirt.*

THE BATH HOUSE had a large exercise yard where people played ball games, lifted weights and wrestled. After exercising, they went to a series of heated rooms to wash and relax.

THE ROOMS and bath water were heated by a furnace stoked by slaves. Hot air from the fire passed through spaces under the floors and inside the walls. The hottest room was the one closest to the furnace.

Once inside, the bathers first went to an icy plunge pool called a *frigidarium*. From there they passed to a warmer room – the *tepidarium*. This was where oils were applied to the skin and then scraped off, so that the bather would be thoroughly clean.

INSTEAD OF SOAP, Romans used olive oil. They rubbed it all over their bodies and scraped it off with a curved metal tool called a *strigil*. Wealthy Romans had personal slave attendants to scrape them down. Poorer Romans had to rub their backs against the walls to scrape the parts they couldn't reach!

FINALLY, THE BATHERS went to a steam room, called a *caldarium*, or to the *laconicum*, or hot room. Then they were clean enough to swim in the swimming pool, or *natatio*. Around the pool there were entertainers, hairdressers and people selling food and drink. Businessmen even held meetings at the baths.

KNUCKLEBONES, or *astragali*, was a popular game at the baths. Players used the small anklebones of a sheep, which have six sides. It was an easy game to play: a player would throw the bones up into the air and try to catch them on the back of the hand. Knucklebones could also be played like dice, with each side of the bones having a different value. Wealthy Romans played with knuckle-bones made from marble, silver or precious stones.

MAKE KNUCKLEBONES

You will need: self-hardening clay, poster paints, paintbrush

1 Mould the clay into 10 knucklebone shapes with 6 sides as shown above.

▽ *Roman girls and women loved to relax at the baths by playing knucklebones.*

2 Paint the knucklebones and give five to each player.

The basic way to play knucklebones is described opposite. Each player should throw in turn. Try and catch as many on the back of your hand as possible. Add up the number of those that you manage to catch.

△ *This mosaic from Pompeii shows actors and musicians getting ready for a performance.*

MASKS were worn in most types of play. These larger-than-life masks showed the sex of the character, as well as his or her mood. Thanks to the masks, the audience could tell at once if an actor was meant to be an angry old man, a comical slave or a beautiful woman. Masks for tragedy showed an expression of horror or despair.

PANTOMIME was a performance in which a single actor mimed several parts, using a series of masks with closed mouths. It was like a solo ballet dance and demanded a great deal of skill. With their faces covered, the actors relied on movement to show their feelings. Pantomime actors were the big stars of the Roman stage.

THEATRE was invented by the Greeks. The Romans borrowed two main types of play from them: the first was tragedy, a serious play showing the sufferings of a great hero or heroine, usually from a Greek myth. The second was comedy, a light-hearted play about everyday life. Many Roman plays were set in Greece and performed by Greek actors.

▽ *This is a mask that a woman might have worn in a tragic play.*

AUDIENCES were often very noisy. People either cheered the actors, or shouted insults at them. The producer of *The Mother-in-Law*, a comedy by Terence, described his lively audience: 'I was successful in holding the audience — at least to the end of the first act. But then a rumour spread that some gladiators were going to perform — and my audience flew off in a huge crowd, pushing, shouting, fighting to get a good spot at the gladiator performance.'

You will need: two lengths of coloured card 6 cm x 90 cm, paint, paintbrush, wool, glue, double-sided sticky tape, a circle of fabric 32 cm in diameter

1 Stick the ends of one of the pieces of card together to make a circle. Stretch the fabric over the circle and glue down tightly around the edges to make the drum.

2 Stick a strip of the tape along the other length of card. Wrap around the drum, sticky side to the fabric.

3 Paint your drum as shown above.

4 Tie together four tassels from your coloured wool and glue them around your drum.

SPECIAL EFFECTS were very popular with Roman audiences. Actors playing gods would swoop across the stage attached to wires. Even horses and carriages appeared in some plays.

△ This kind of drum was often used in Roman theatre.

MUSIC was very important in the theatre. Musicians played the pipes, trumpets, cymbals and drums, while the actors sang songs. Although we know what instruments were played, we have no way of knowing what Roman music sounded like.

◁ This actor is wearing a comic mask. Actors used masks and hand gestures to show different characters.

Amazing architects

The Romans were among the best builders in history. They built things that served practical purposes, such as canals, bridges, sewers, harbours and roads. But it was perhaps in constructing aqueducts that their engineering skills were most impressive.

▽ *Rome was served by eight aqueducts, each built using wooden scaffolding such as this.*

△ *This Roman aqueduct still stands in Segovia, in central Spain.*

covered water channel

AQUEDUCTS were developed by the Romans. They are channels for carrying water that were mostly dug into the earth, following the contours of hills. Where this was not possible, the Romans built arches made of concrete and stone. It took great skill to build an aqueduct. The water channel had to slope at exactly the right angle all the way along its length, to give a steady flow of water.

AN ARCH is a curved structure which is able to support great weight. By using arches, the Romans found they could build high, strong walls using as little stone as possible.

CONCRETE was also a Roman invention. It was a mixture of volcanic sand and stone rubble, held together by mortar made from lime and water. It was strong, cheap and much easier to use than stone blocks. Concrete and arches made it possible to build structures like the Colosseum.

PLINY THE ELDER described the work involved in giving Rome its water supply: 'If we think of the abundant supply of water for public buildings, baths, settling tanks, pools, private houses, gardens and country estates close to the city; and of the distance the water travels, the height of the arches, the tunnelling through mountains, the levelling of routes across deep valleys; we can only conclude that this is a supreme wonder of the world.'

▷ *This surveyor is using a* **groma** *– a wooden cross mounted on a pole, with weighted strings at the ends which hung vertically.*

wooden scaffolding supports arches as they are being built

THE SURVEYOR was the person who marked out the ground before building. To plot right angles, he used an instrument called a *groma*. The surveyor took sightings along each of the arms of the cross using assistants who stood in the distance. He signalled to his assistants to move either left or right, so that they lined up. Then they laid out a long straight line of flags.

GOOD ROADS helped the Romans to expand their empire. Armies had to be able to move from place to place as quickly as possible with all their equipment. Before the Romans, roads were muddy tracks that were almost impossible to use in wet weather, especially for wheeled transport. The Romans made paved roads that could be used almost all year round. The surface was curved so that rainwater would drain off into ditches at the edges. Roman roads were usually as straight as possible, even if this sometimes meant tunnelling through a cliff.

Feeding the Empire

Some of the best farmland in the Roman Empire was along the coast of North Africa. The soil there was good and the climate was excellent, with long, hot summers and regular rain in winter. It was the perfect place for growing wheat – in fact, North Africa produced two-thirds of the grain eaten in Rome.

△ *This fourth-century mosaic shows farm labourers gathering and treading grapes.*

ROMAN FARMS were often enormous and were owned by very wealthy people. In the first century AD, half of North Africa was said to belong to just six men. Roman landlords spent most of their time in the cities, living extravagantly. They either rented the land out to tenants, or left their farms in the hands of a bailiff who was in charge of a gang of slaves.

FARM BUILDINGS included barns for storing grain and straw, stables for the animals, and various workshops – a blacksmith's forge for making and repairing tools, and a pottery for making storage jars. There were buildings for pressing grapes and olives, and a mill for grinding wheat. The type and quality of crops grown varied throughout the Empire. Olives could be grown only in the warm south. Grapes were grown in southern Britain, but they were not as good as those from Spain or Italy.

RELIGIOUS CEREMONIES played a big part in the farmers' year. The Romans believed that ceremonies were just as important as sowing or ploughing at the right time. In May, for example, a pig, a ram and a bull were led around the boundaries of the fields and then killed as a sacrifice to the god Mars. The farmer would say, 'Father Mars, I pray that you keep disease and bad weather away from my fields and that you allow my harvest, my corn and my vineyard to flourish.'

▷ *A Roman farm on the north coast of Africa.*

team of oxen harnessed to a mechanical harvester

beehives

wheat

OLIVE TREES were grown all over North Africa, but the olives from Tripolitania (present-day Libya) were particularly famous. They were grown on dry hillsides, above fields of wheat. The olives could either be eaten, or crushed in an oil press for their rich oil.

SLAVES did most of the farm work. A trusted slave called a *vilicus* was in charge of the field labourers. They had to work very hard, if not, they might be beaten or kept in chains. Farm work was used as a punishment for town slaves whose masters thought they were lazy.

▷ *Farmers' tools were simple but effective. These knives were used for pruning grapevines.*

stables

olive press

farmhouse *or* villa rustica

slaves' quarters

olive grove

livestock

Trade and transport

Wherever they went, the Roman armies built roads. Although they were for military use, Roman roads made it easier to transport goods on carts pulled by mules and oxen, no matter what the weather. Heavy goods were moved by water wherever possible, along rivers on barges pulled by oxen, or across the sea on merchant ships.

THE PEACE that was brought by Roman rule helped trade to flourish from one end of the Empire to the other. The demands of the wealthy also meant that luxury goods, such as silks and spices, were brought from distant lands.

△ *Coins were used throughout the Empire.*

WITHIN THE EMPIRE, the most important trade was in metals, luxury goods, and foods such as wine, olive oil, grain and fish sauce.

Some goods were imported from beyond the Empire. Silk came from as far away as China along an overland route called the Silk Road. Spices for cooking were brought by sea from India, and incense, which the Romans burned on the altars of the gods, came overland from southern Arabia by camel caravans, or by ships sailing up the Red Sea.

KEY TO TRADE MAP

wild animals   *wild animals*   *slaves*   *corn*   *wine*   *oil*   *gold*   *metals*

▽ *This map shows where some of the goods traded around the Empire came from.*

BRITANNIA

GERMANIA

GAUL

IBERIA

ANATOLIA

DALMATIA

Rome

ITALIA

SYRIA

MACEDONIA

Mediterranean Sea

MAURETANIA

AFRICA

CYRENAICA   AEGYPTUS   *Red Sea*

△ *Traders made healthy profits from transporting exotic animals around the Empire.*

◉ ✳ **PLINY THE ELDER** thought that foreign luxury goods were costing the Empire too much: 'At the lowest reckoning, India, China and Arabia carry off one hundred million *sestertii* a year from our Empire – such is the bill for our pleasures and our ladies.'

WILD ANIMALS were brought from all parts of the Empire and from lands beyond for the games in Rome. Bears were shipped from Scotland and Ireland. Elephants came from Africa and India.

◉ ✳ **THE SAME COINS** were used throughout the Empire which made trading simple. The basic unit was a copper coin called an *as*. A larger copper coin, called the *dupondius*, was worth 2 asses; a bronze coin, the *sestertius*, was worth 4 asses; a silver *denarius* equalled 16 asses; and a gold *aureus* was worth 100 asses.

◉ ✳ **A ROMAN COIN** was like a tiny newspaper in some ways. One side was used by the emperor to announce important events, such as a military victory. He also used coins to try to win people's support. The coin might show him speaking to his troops – giving people the impression that he was in firm command. Another coin might show the emperor as the chief priest, so that people would think that the gods were behind him.

▷ *A merchant weighs some fruit using a set of scales.*

lead weight in the shape of a head

SHIPS were used to move people and goods around the Empire and beyond. As well as travelling for trade and religious reasons, some wealthy Romans went sightseeing, and some even had guidebooks.

▽ *A Roman war galley.*

sail was lowered
before going
into battle

underwater
battering ram

up to five men
manned each oar

WAR GALLEYS were slim, fast vessels. They were powered by oarsmen who sat on benches below deck, pulling in time to orders shouted by the helmsman. At the bow, or front, there was a battering ram made from wood covered in bronze. Galleys would try to ram enemy ships in the side. Then the crew of marines (naval soldiers) would jump on board the enemy ship for hand-to-hand fighting.

PIRATES were a menace in the first century BC. Fleets of pirates based in the eastern Mediterranean raided coastal towns and seized any ships they could. They stole the cargoes and held the crews for ransom, or sold them as slaves. In 67 BC, the Romans gathered a fleet of war galleys and hunted the pirates down to make the sea safe.

THE SAILING SEASON lasted from March to November. Few ships put to sea in winter because of the risk of storms, and because of shorter daylight hours. However, the city of Rome needed wheat grown abroad to feed its people, so some huge grain ships had to make the dangerous winter journey from North Africa. When grain supplies ran low in the granaries, there was panic in Rome.

IN THE SECOND CENTURY AD, the Greek writer Lucian described the *Isis*, one of the great grain ships that sailed out of Egypt: 'What a big ship! About 180 feet [55 metres] long and something over a quarter of that wide… And then the height of the mast! And how the stern rises with its gentle curve, with its golden beak, balanced at the opposite end by the long rising length of the prow, with a figure of the goddess Isis on either side!'

▽ *Merchant ships carried people, food supplies and wild animals for the games.*

yard

foresail, or
steering sail

MERCHANT SHIPS were used to move goods around the Empire. These ships were large and round-bellied, to provide lots of storage space for all the sacks of grain and *amphorae*, or pottery jars, holding oil or wine. Because of their shape, these ships were stable but very slow. They had a big square sail on the mast with a smaller sail at the bow. Two large oars at the stern, or rear, were used for steering.

central mast

THE DANGERS of sea travel are shown by the many Roman shipwrecks that have been found around the Mediterranean. Some still have their ancient cargo of oil and wine preserved in *amphorae*.

mainsail

flag and carved swan's head

forestay

anchor   *cargo hold*

steering oar

hull made of pine, cypress or elder wood

The Roman army

In the first century AD, the Roman army was mostly made up of legionaries and auxiliaries. There were 28 legions, mainly stationed around the borders of the Empire. Each one had a number and a name that was either a nickname or the place where the troops were raised. For example, the sixth legion was called *Victrix*, or victorious, and the ninth legion was called *Hispana*, or Spanish.

lionskin headdress worn over a helmet

◁ *A legionary from the first century BC.*

A LEGIONARY was a Roman foot soldier. On marches, they had to carry heavy loads of weapons, tools and supplies. If they were not fighting or training, legionaries had to do building work. They cut down trees, quarried stone, and built roads, bridges and forts.

▽ *A Syrian archer of the early second century AD.*

Syrian archers wore long robes

△ *An aquilifer from the first century AD.*

AUXILIARIES were soldiers who came from the provinces and who were not Roman citizens. They were poorly paid, earning only a third of the legionaries' rate. Auxiliaries fought using the familiar weapons of their own countries. Cavalrymen came from Gaul (France) and North Africa, slingers from islands off Spain, and archers from Syria. Auxiliaries supplied the extra fighting skills that the legions lacked.

◊ **THE AQUILIFER,** or eagle bearer, carried the standard of the legion – a golden eagle on a pole. Smaller units also had standards, such as golden hands or busts of the emperor. These were used to rally the soldiers in battle. Aquilifers had to be very brave, for they led the men into the most dangerous places on the battlefield. The lionskins on their helmets were a symbol of their rank and courage.

long spear used for stabbing from horseback

▽ *A cavalry officer from the fourth century AD.*

silver-plated helmet

▷ *A centurion from the middle of the first century AD.*

helmet with sideways crest

🦅 ◊ **EACH LEGION** had around 5,500 soldiers, including 120 horsemen who acted as messengers and scouts, keeping an eye on the enemy. The rest of the soldiers were divided into small units called centuries, each of about 80 men. Six centuries grouped together made a cohort.

silver and gold medals on chest

vine cane used to point at, or beat, the men

◊ **A CENTURION** was an officer in charge of a century. To show his rank, he wore special armour made from silver-coloured metal scales and shiny greaves (shin guards). He also wore a helmet with a sideways crest as a sign of his status. He kept his men in order by beating them with a vine cane, either as a punishment, or to make them work harder.

✳ **CAVALRYMEN** played an even more important role during the later Empire, when large armies of soldiers on horseback fought alongside the legions, defending the Empire. By the fourth century, the cavalry carried long swords and round shields.

LEGIONARIES were full-time soldiers. They joined the army at about the age of 18, and had to serve for the next 20 to 25 years. It was a hard life, but it also offered security and regular pay to the poorest Roman citizens. Through good service, legionaries might be promoted to the rank of centurion. If they survived the battles they fought, they could retire and live a comfortable life.

New recruits had to swear an oath that they were free-born Roman citizens, not slaves. Sometimes, slaves tried to join the legions. If they were discovered, they were executed.

DRILLING AND MARCHING took up a large part of the legionaries' day. In his book *Military Service*, the author Vegetius described the type of training programme that legionaries were put through: 'Every recruit, without exception, should in the summer months learn to swim, for it is not always possible to cross rivers on bridges… They should be accustomed also to leap and strike blows at the same time, to rise up with a bound and sink down again behind the shield… They must also practise throwing their javelins at the posts from a distance to increase their skill in aiming, and the strength of the arm.'

MAKE A PAIR OF ARMOURED SHOES

You will need: scissors, chicken wire, paper, string, flour, water, salt, paint

1 Ask an adult to help you mould the chicken wire to fit the top of your feet.

2 Make a runny paste of flour and water. Add a pinch of salt. Cover the shapes (inside and out) in layers of strips of paper dipped in the paste. Leave them to dry.

3 Cut off the tops of the toes as shown to make toe shields.

4 Cut four 8 cm lengths of string. Use paper and paste to fix the string to the underside of each foot cover and the toe shields. Paint the shields as shown.

5 Make two small holes in the sides of each shoe. Thread string through the holes and tie around your ankles.

PUNISHMENTS were harsh in the army. Soldiers who fell asleep on guard duty or who ran away in battle were stoned to death. If a whole unit showed cowardice or refused to obey orders, it could be punished with decimation, which meant that one man in every ten was killed.

However, life was not all bad for a Roman soldier. At Vindolanda, a Roman fort in northern Britain, archaeologists found many letters written on thin sheets of wood. In one letter, dating from AD 120, a soldier complains that his unit has run out of beer!

▷ *This is a copy of foot armour that was found in the south of Italy, in an early Greek settlement.*

BAGGAGE MULES trotted alongside the marching soldiers. There was one mule for every eight men. It carried a leather tent and a millstone for grinding corn. Other mules were loaded with dismantled catapults, used for hurling stones at the enemy.

supplies carried on a wooden cross on the legionary's back

cooking pots

A JAVELIN, or *pilum*, had a long metal tip that bent on impact. This meant that the enemy could not throw it back. Soldiers fought in tight formation, obeying trumpet signals. After throwing their javelins, they drew their short swords and thrust at the enemy from behind their shields.

WHEN ATTACKING an enemy stronghold, soldiers grouped together and covered themselves with their shields for protection. This defence was called 'the tortoise'. The men gathered into a square and those at the edges linked their curved shields together to make a wall of wood. The men in the middle held their shields above their heads to make a roof. This kept them safe from enemy missiles.

▽ *An early legionary shown with the equipment he was expected to carry on long marches.*

cloak

water pouch

turf cutter

mattock for building camp

javelin, or pilum

spear

wooden shield carried on legionary's back

The fall of Rome

In the fourth century AD, the Roman Empire was weakened by a series of invasions. German tribes poured over the Rhine and Danube rivers. To meet the threat, the Roman Empire was split into two halves. There was an emperor in the west, sometimes ruling from Rome, and another in the east ruling from Constantinople (Istanbul) in Turkey.

✴ **ROME WAS CAPTURED** and plundered in AD 410 by Alaric, king of a German people. The news of the fall of the city shocked the Roman world. Jerome, a monk in Palestine, wrote to a friend: 'Terrifying news has come to us from the West. Rome has been taken by assault… My voice is still and sobs disturb my every utterance. The city has been conquered which had once controlled the entire world.'

△ *Many tourists visit the remains of the Colosseum in Rome.*

THE GERMAN INVADERS set up their own kingdoms in Western Europe. One group, the Franks, settled in Gaul and became the French. Other German peoples, the Saxons and Angles, settled in Britain and became the English. The invaders did not usually want to destroy the Roman Empire. As a result, many aspects of the Roman way of life were kept alive in Western Europe.

▷ *The title 'Caesar' was used by the emperors, from Augustus to Hadrian, and by other powerful rulers throughout history.*

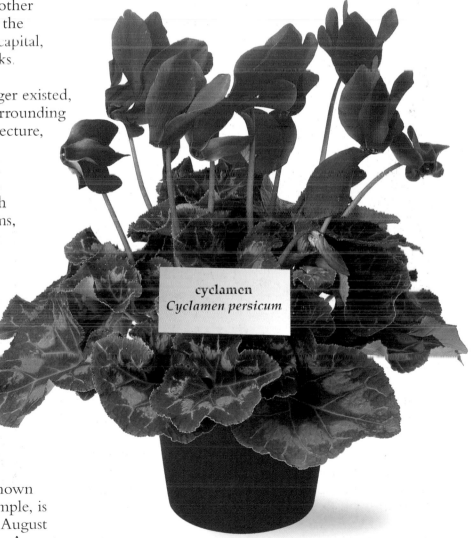

◁ *The eagle, once the symbol of the Roman Empire, is now a symbol of the USA and appears on the one-dollar bill. For the Romans, the eagle was the king of birds and represented Jupiter, the king of the gods, and god of the sky.*

ROMAN POLITICS AND LAW have had a lasting influence. The USA has modelled its system of government on the Roman Republic and adopted the eagle as a national emblem. Throughout history, many rulers have looked to the power and inspiration of the emperors and the Roman Empire. In some countries, rulers adopted the title 'Caesar': in Russia, it became 'Tzar', and in Germany it became 'Kaiser'.

THE EASTERN EMPIRE survived for another thousand years. It was only in 1453 that the last eastern emperor died defending his capital, Constantinople, against the Muslim Turks.

By the 16th century the Empire no longer existed, but its influence lived on in the lands surrounding the Mediterranean in the form of architecture, language, literature and government.

ROMAN ARCHITECTURE still influences modern buildings. Public buildings, such as banks, libraries, churches and museums, are often modelled on Roman temples, with tall, decorative columns.

THE LATIN LANGUAGE developed into French, Italian, Spanish, Portuguese and Romanian. Pure Latin was kept alive in church services and writings. It also became, with Greek, an international language for scientists who classify plants, animals and parts of the body using Latin names.

THE MONTHS OF THE YEAR are still known by their Roman names. March, for example, is named after the Roman god Mars, and August gets its name from Rome's first emperor, Augustus. The planets are also named after Roman gods.

cyclamen
Cyclamen persicum

△ *Latin is used to classify plants and species of animals.*

Glossary

amphitheatre An oval-shaped Roman building without a roof. It was used for public shows, such as fights between gladiators and wild animals.

amphora A tall pottery vase with two handles used for transporting and storing wine, olive oil, vinegar and fish sauce.

aqueduct An artificial channel, made of stone and concrete, used for carrying water from one area to another.

archaeologist Someone who searches for and studies the remains of past times, such as ancient buildings and artefacts.

atrium The entrance hall of a Roman house.

augur A religious official whose job was to find out whether the gods approved or disapproved of a course of action. The augur did this by watching the flight and behaviour of birds. No important decisions were made in Rome without consulting the sacred flock of chickens.

auxiliary Soldiers drawn from the non-citizen population of the Empire. They were paid less than citizen soldiers. On retirement, they became Roman citizens.

barbarian A word used by the Greeks and Romans to describe foreigners.

centurion A middle-ranking Roman officer in charge of a 'century' of men (80).

Chi-Rho (pronounced ky-roh) A sign used by early Christians to show their faith. It combines the Greek letters X (Chi) and P (Rho), the first two letters of the word Christ.

circus An oval track for chariot races. The most famous was the Circus Maximus in Rome.

citizen A citizen of the Roman Empire was a full member of the Roman state, and had more rights than a non-citizen.

civilization A developed and organized group of people or nation. The Romans believed that civilization was marked by town life, laws, reading and writing, and religious ceremonies.

client A person who owed loyalty to a wealthier Roman, who was their patron.

consul The most important Roman government official. Two consuls were elected each year.

early imperial period The period of Roman history from 27 BC to AD 284. For most of this time, the Empire was ruled by the emperor.

emperor The ruler of the Roman Empire. The rule of the emperors was known as imperial rule.

equestrian A member of a class of wealthy Roman citizens. Each equestrian owned a personal fortune of at least 400,000 sestertii.

Etruscans The people who lived in north-west Italy in ancient times. The Etruscans were an important influence on the Romans.

fasces A bundle of rods, tied around an axe, and an Etruscan symbol of power, adopted by the Romans.

forum The central market-place and public meeting area in every Roman town.

freedmen and freedwomen Slaves who bought or were given their freedom. If their former owners were Roman citizens, they became citizens too. However, they did not have as many rights as free-born citizens.

fresco A type of wall painting in which paint is applied to damp plaster.

gladiator A man who fought in the arena, either against another gladiator, or an animal. Gladiators were mostly slaves, although those that were successful were able to buy their freedom.

groma A tool used by Roman surveyors to plot straight lines, right-angles and grids.

haruspice A religious official whose job was to predict the future or to find out the wishes of the gods. He did this by inspecting the inner organs of sacrificed animals. He also interpreted lightning and unusual events in nature, such as earthquakes.

insula A block of housing in a Roman town.

Isis An important Egyptian goddess worshipped by the Romans. She was seen by her followers as the queen of the whole universe. Isis also had specific roles as a goddess of wheat and barley, childbirth, and seafarers.

late imperial period The period of Roman history from AD 284 to 476. For most of this period, the Empire was divided into two halves. It also became a Christian empire.

Latin The language spoken by the Romans and the other peoples of Latium, an area in central Italy. The ancient people of Latium were called Latins.

legionary A Roman citizen who served as an infantry soldier in a legion.

magistrate An elected official who governed the Roman state. Under the Republic, the most powerful officials were the two consuls. There were also the praetors, who were in charge of justice, and the quaestors, who looked after state money.

Mithras A god of light, first worshipped in Persia, and later, in secret, by men throughout the Roman Empire.

mosaic A picture made from hundreds of tiny pieces of pottery, stone or glass tiles, pressed into cement.

pater familias The father and head of a Roman family.

province A large area of the Roman Empire ruled by its own governor.

provincial A native of one of the provinces of the Roman Empire. Provincials had fewer rights than citizens, but were much better off than slaves.

Roman Empire The different lands and peoples ruled by the Romans. 'The Empire' also means the period when Rome was ruled by emperors, rather than by elected officials.

Roman Republic A period when Rome and the Empire were ruled by elected officials.

senators A member of the senate, a council of leading nobles who advised the consuls and the Emperor. In the Empire, senators commanded the armies and governed provinces. To be a senator, you had to be elected as a member of the magistrates, and have a huge personal fortune of at least a million sestertii.

shrine A place where holy objects, such as statues of gods, were placed and worshipped. Many Romans had shrines in their homes.

standard bearer Someone who carried a pole with a flag, metal eagle or a placard on the top. Standards were used in religious processions, and as rallying points for soldiers in battle.

strigil A curved metal tool that was used at the Roman baths for scraping oil and dirt off skin

stylus A pen-like instrument used for writing on wax tablets.

symbol A sign, or an object that stands for something else, is said to be a symbol. For example, a cross is a symbol of Christianity; a lionskin headdress is a symbol of bravery.

tablinum A Roman reception room.

toga A gown worn by Roman citizens. It was made of a single woollen sheet and wrapped around the body.

triclinium A Roman dining room with three couches in an open square for guests to lie upon.

Index